Something Beautiful Travels Far

POEMS

SHAISTA TAYABALI

© 2018, Text by Shaista Tayabali
© 2018, Illustrations by Shaista Tayabali
About The Author photo by Chris Boland

All rights reserved. Except for brief quotations in critical articles or reviews, no part of this book may be reproduced in any manner without prior written permission from the author.
www.lupusinflight.com

Copyright © Shaista Tayabali 2018

ISBN-10: 1725862654
ISBN-13: 978-1725862654

For Mary

Who brings me joy and makes me laugh.
A hundred more years would not be enough.

Poems

I, daughter, of monsoon rains
Crocuses	13
Something Beautiful Travels Far	14
Portrait of An Artist's Daughter	15
Hanami Sakura	18
Solace	19

Just another case of girl, interrupted
Exuberance	23
The Blood of Trees	24
Girl, Interrupted	25
Shaista	26
Butterflies	27

Love letters in orange and gold
All This And Heaven Too	31
The Year of Yes	32
Tegalalang	33
The Gathering	35
Bruges: Diary of an Escaping Poet	36
Nippon, Watashi Wa Anatani Utaimassu	38

Sometimes you have to catch the light
A Walking Poem for Thich Nhat Hanh	41
Ode to a Tiny Flowerpot	43
Moving Plates	44
Summer Solstice	45

Touching Time	46
Faded Patchwork	47

I followed stardust and scalpel stones

Taking Strawberry Hibiscus Tea	51
Sweet Little Lies	53
Night of the Blood Moon	55
The Book of Books	56
Yuki-san	57
The Art of War	58

Hold still, my whirling dervishes

Women in a Waiting Room	61
Cataract	62
Scintillating Scotoma	63
The Man Who Prints Eyeballs	64
Sunday Sweep	66

I took the quiet road

Nirbhaya	69
Tattered Wings	70
Blade of Green	71
A Poet Said	72
After the Rain	73

About the Author   75

Something Beautiful Travels Far

I, daughter, of monsoon rains

Crocuses

My father knows when
the crocuses are out

and when the snowdrops
and when the bluebells

and how to listen, carefully,
to the nesting birds

trilling
between our rooms.

Daisies will come
and roses will grow

and perhaps we shall walk
and reminisce about the snow

and kick up some leaves
and weave up some dreams

while the world passes by
my father and I.

Something Beautiful Travels Far

I fall into a cup of tea,
with all my heart;
the sun comes out,
to join me.

Blue flowers on bone china,
all the way from Bengal;
something beautiful travels far,
to be present on my palm.

On my arm a glinting thing,
a golden watch, a hanging charm;
a golden bangle, worn and fine,
from my great-great-grandmother's skin

to mine.

Portrait of An Artist's Daughter

She was crafty, the whole school knew:
in the silences, we watched her creations,
spring from nothing,
into Holi designs.

Chalk-powder, linseed oil,
apron, palette-knife;
fingertips scraping paints into place,
high ridges I can still trace

with today's hands,
because the work travelled with her,
past religious riots, over oceans,
and into the gallery of a new home
where I have my own room:

a black and white mural
begun, unfinished, on my wall.
I spend my first weeks contemplating
stamps that will stake MINE.

Not the family motto from her side though:
that will always rankle.
This Too Shall Pass.
We moved from light to dark, and cold,
from fear to being feared –
this chaos was meant to be?

In the kitchen, the other artist:
the white stick walker,
anxiety-bearer, worrier, ex-sorcerer,
one who could read the bones.
The diagnostic who could not diagnose

his own daughter,
leans weary, looks back in angst
to stars and lunar unknowns,
trying to unlearn radiology, replace it
with astronomy.

We are all looking for guidelines
to sew the fault lines together.
I, daughter, remember the clean, double
break of radius and ulna,
the colour of white heat,
and bloodless red,

like when two sharp stones meet
to strike fire.

I, daughter, of monsoon rains
and carom games,
rode ancient elephants,
hid from sacred bulls,
hearing terror in oilskin drums,

gathering gulmohar,
adorned by magnolia,
only to become invisible,
as though the artist
took eraser in thumb
and scrubbed
        rubbed

                me out.

Hanami Sakura

I have missed the flowering
of the cherry tree

falling petals rain down on me
a carpet of white and mossy green;

I am soaring high to the furthest trees
with the kissing bees and the singing birds

and swooping down with the lowering sky
to brush the earth with clouds of skirt.

Solace

If I should die tomorrow
there would be many sorrows
but the deeper print of my name
would carry you through the pain

and if you should hear me laugh
I am only playing a game
hold on, hold on to the centre
till I find my way again.

Just another case of girl, interrupted

Exuberance

I have high fevers and night sweats.
My fingers and toes flush hot and cold,

and transform
into purple flowers.

My face, that transient thing,
breaking up and taking shape,

a sweet moon
in a thunder cloud sky.

In moments of perfect beauty,
my face reveals its grace.

Lupus, you odd unnatural thing,
I am razing you to the ground.

Here, on the ward, I am laughing,
I am offering my exuberant soul.

Take it,
if you dare.

The Blood of Trees

I lie,
fallen tree.

Yesterday, they
cut a hole in me
three needles thick.

They read my paper skin
in Braille and rust
and bone.

They sucked my limbs
of milk and marrow
and when I cried for home

they sought my neck,
pale birch, fat jugular,
and drove their cannula in.

Girl, Interrupted

The gleaming pebble
from my sparkly days

rubs itself raw
and ruinous

here, on the stroke unit,
I am just another case

of Girl, Interrupted.

I have lost my face
along the waterways

of little deaths,
and unbearable truths.

I have lost my place,
lost the fluidity of my grace.

Shaista

'Shaista.
That is a proud name,' he said.

I am proud of my name.

It is the Rajput name for warriors.
It is the Persian name for poets.

Am I not then Shaista, the warrior-poet?

I am standing on the battleground,
listing a little,
sword and pen at the ready,
blood and words aplenty.

But I long for sakura,
snow pink petals of my cherry tree.

Oh brief, beautiful one,
wrap yourself around me,

so I can be Shaista, the free.

Butterflies

We are aged and ageless,
together on the ward,
blending blue,
against a dull stone sky.

We are a strange alien race,
hooked to wires, trailing machines,
tangled in each other's space.
We smile: quirky twists of face.

I long for a bed, a blanket, a cushion,
heat, sand, beach, oblivion.

Outside the windows, a playground
I have never seen children in;
a chessboard with giant squares,
and no chessmen.

The light has faded to black now.
I turn to the faces within,
to patches of white and yellow butterflies,
tucked securely into skin.

Love letters in orange and gold

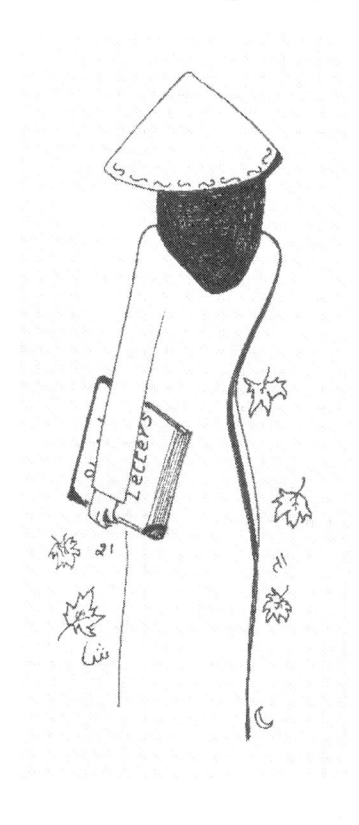

All This And Heaven Too

Autumn breathes outside a window
in a garden I knew before.

Ripe colours I knew
in a different form.

Love letters in orange and gold
trying to find their way to free me.

The Year of Yes
(for Victoria)

I wish I had said *yes*!
beloved,
when you asked me out to walk,

among the leaves, the turning leaves,
you were offering me
the sound of dreams,

and I turned you down, politely.
Not today, I smiled.
Perhaps, maybe, tomorrow?

But I wish I had said *yes*!
beloved,
I wish we had shared this light.

Next time, don't ask,
just take me.
Order me to dress!

I am going to need your help,
beloved,
to begin the year of yes.

Tegalalang
(for Theresa)

My heart gives out
on the way to the paddy fields.

Dragonflies the size of birds
circle the rice and visit me
in my bamboo cave.

What can be heard
but not seen:
    the song of mosquitoes
    enjoying me.

In Bas we make an accidental stop
to taste coffee expelled by the Luak monkey:
most expensive in the world!
    a tray of coffees and teas
    to tempt palate and wallet

but here, at this height,
we are wealthy enough,
and soon heady drunk enough
    on Arabica and Robusta
    for anything.

We take a different route, you and I,
when we pass through archways,

or slip inside doorways,

but we always meet
on the other side.

The Gathering
(for Liv & Marian)

Give me peat fires
and candles lit
at the Church of Mercy.

Give me soft haze of blue
mountains and sharp edges of ice
on our way to Conor Pass.

Give me Dingle
and Slea Head
and blue butterflies on Inch Strand Beach.

Stop at Fermoyle
after kissing the Stone
then touch the sands of Dún Chaoin.

Time is a dandelion,
but not the land,
she is constant –

waiting, waiting,
for the gathering,
of the poet and her clan.

Bruges: Diary of an Escaping Poet
(for Angelina)

On a train all aboard
Cambridge to London Kings.
No camera in my pocket.

Only paper, pens,
and the lively curiosity
of a mind ready for travel.

We jet in and out of tunnels
waiting patiently for light.
And after Lille, the sun,

wide open space of green,

and the sweet forgetful vulnerability
of a girl on a birthday spree,
escaping, free.

Under the dome of a Basilisk sky
pitted with cloud
and the charge of knights,

a brusque and brutal sun
patronises the teeming hordes,
the hungry leonine summer hordes,

while the captive saints brood,
mourning quieter days.

Brugge waking up,

>	washing her streets,
>	readying her lace,
>	sugaring her waffles;

we leave
with little trace.

Nippon, Watashi Wa Anatani Utaimassu
(Japan, I Sing To You)

The willow bloomed just yesterday,
in green and yellow plumes;
my father heard its Circe song
and listening, listening, walked on.

The sky opened, all bright and light,
the earth caressed his feet;
in Sendai a tsunami burst
beneath many fathers' feet.

Such wings we need when our planes fall,
such wings we need when our earth calls
us to attention;

listening, listening, to fire and storm,
trying to sing our wingless songs
and make a good impression.

Sometimes you have to catch the light

A Walking Poem for Thich Nhat Hanh
(and for Dr. Ho)

I bought a treadmill.
What would Thây say?

Would he smile and shake his head
or look bemused the way he looked

the day I waited in line to ask
a question that did not need answering?

The birds are busy and my shoe is broken
and my foot turns in to awkward positions.

My unfocused eyes make nausea
of the green world around me.

Oh dappled light, what would Thây say?
Walk outside!

Thây, who is struggling to sit upright,
is recovering from the stroke,

which left him paralysed and comatose.
Oh Venerable One, who took three months

to drink a quarter cup of tea,

who watched the full moon patiently,

like when he was sixteen,
and Têt promised endless treats

of moon cakes and dragon dance
and calligraphic Buddha chants.

Oh Patient Impermanent One,
these broken steps are made for you;

these perfect steps I make for you
make me free.

Ode to a Tiny Flowerpot
(for Mary)

In some part of me I must believe
nothing can be broken.
What else explains this carelessness?

It was the tiniest clay pot,
made for seeds and
the tiniest tree.

I am manifesting it whole
in this poem, so it knows
it was loved the way it was,

but also the way it is
now, exposed innards,
cracked through.

Someone will put you together,
I tell the flowerpot, and myself.
Mostly, I tell myself.

Moving Plates
(for Annette)

The perfect home
has something sentimental
resting side by side with the practical.

Everything a meaning,
a memory,
a moment –

even the broken,
the chipped china,
but especially the handwoven,

crochet craftwork,
and the little notes
you write yourself.

You leave for us
   a forget-me-not trail
        winding all the way

  to 1939
when the plates
  of your atlas

             moved forever.

Summer Solstice

The clematis are dying
in purple paper clusters,

a pretty, dusty, crepuscular fading
of old lace,

doilies,
beside the newly hatched delphinium –

only the daisies seem invincible.

Touching Time

Tucked away inside a wooden cabinet, I find
The Tibetan Book of Living and Dying.

Books can save your life. Some say
they can even help you die.

In Stanley Park, I stand inside
a dead tree;
a hollowed out by time tree;
a rescued by man, propped up by iron tree:

I feel nothing.

You are touching time, my mother observes,
but the tree says nothing to me.

Faded Patchwork
(for Vera Mama)

Sometimes you have to catch
the light, just where it falls

beyond the line of blue iris
and purple clematis,
to where the oak tree stands boundary.

Shade comes too soon, and the blanket
wrapped around your knees reminds you
of the ages yet to come.

An old knit, still holding true
everywhere, except for two

black squares eaten away,
which remind you
the knitter is gone too.

I followed stardust and scalpel stones

Taking Strawberry Hibiscus Tea with Strangers

On a Tuesday afternoon
in the only place to be,
tables must be shared, politely.

I join the ladies at Number 5
and flash a half-mast smile,
not the full-watt,

(they have been here a while);
they fall silent with a proprietary air
and watch me settle.

The mug and saucer are mottled grey
ceramic, but surprisingly light
as I lift my fruit and flower

blush pink drink to my lips
and for once feel happy
with my choice.

The Jackson Five count out the alphabet
behind cutlery,
and the humming of refrigeration;

I keep my legs firmly crossed
lest they break out, break dance,

break the surface charm
of a genteel English deli.
But the coffee here is Italian
and my tea came from the hibiscus tree;

I remember the flowers falling
and my bare feet rushing
to catch them
before the monsoon floods did.

Sweet Little Lies

You buy cupcakes with your cappuccino
and the barista asks after your love life.

You play dumb and ask after his.
(You overheard him and his friend
– the coffee drinker before you –
discussing how she played him).

He breaks it down scene by scene –
how he went to her birthday and
bought her Millie's Cookies
and everything
but then she never bothered
to show up to his
after he took her out to lunch
and paid
and everything.

And then he turns to you,
till rung up, and chatting
about the single scene,

as though I might be prowling,
and buying cupcakes
in exchange for dates,
might just be my thing.

I deflect, and pick my way
over to a solitary table,
and scald my tongue
on the first bitter sip
before the chocolate lacing soothes it.

What if I told him the reason I was single?
That my body was a battlefield
and my flesh destined for needles
and my eyes a network of scar tissue
and how pain can become the glue?

But later, when two girls come by,
and I hear them giggling together,

I trace the tip of vanilla butterfly wings
and drench my tongue in lemon curd
and let the chocolate orange sing to me

and be glad the only thing he heard
was that I was free.

Night of the Blood Moon

I went to the place where the wild things are,
last night on the trail of the blood moon;
I followed stardust and scalpel stones
to the place beside the runes.

I held my palms, out,
for all the readers to see,
to make what they could
of the threads that bind me
behind the smudging
    and the tearing
    and the rearranging
of my soul.

The blood moon passed over.
I was bathed in blood.
I paid in pain of a different sort,
from a different source,

from the place where the wild things are,
to the place where the unspeakables are,
to the place where the silent are
remembering.

The Book of Books

Open the book of life, and look back
and forward, to the places
where the choices were made.

Sit somewhere,
in a patch of sun,
perhaps.

You made the beauty gather
here,
and here.

And there,
where the threads unravel,
lie the mysteries.

Yuki-san

Yuki, the cherry tree
is quietly blooming now,
but the wind is so impatient
some petals are floating down.

Yesterday, my mother and I
stood in the doorway,
watching the willow.

Green leaves are perfect in spring.

Today, the scent of rain is here.

I am drinking hot tea
sweet with memories,
and listening to birds sing.

Yuki, the cherry is empty now,
the wind stole all the petals,
but the earth is full
with warm, white snow,

and I know you will return soon.

The Art of War
(for Jeanne-ming)

The art of war requires armour and light.
The enemy is more difficult to find in shadow
and stealth is not the style of the true hero.

Rather meet on the white playing field,
where red blood shall melt
in the silence of snow.

And who shall take the lead?
Why, only the true hero.

Hold still, my whirling dervishes

Women in a Waiting Room

Women in a waiting room
dress well for the occasion.
Summer bags and glad rags
and other fashion must haves.

No one would guess
the seething frustration,
the multiplied irritation,
of being women, in a waiting room.

Cataract

I live inside a cataract,
in a dim and shrinking world.

Peel back the blinds! I bellow,
but the clouds just don't hear.

I live inside a lymph node,
(a mean and shotty mass);

I try to kiss it, to calm it,
to shrink it,

but the node just thinks me absurd.

Scintillating Scotoma
(for Dr. Meyer)

Let me see if I can make
poetry out of this.
Let me see if I can whisk
fear out of this.

Scintillating Scotoma.
I like the way it fits
the visual fire,
the zig zagging, iridescent,
shimmering quagmire
of this.

Hold still,
my whirling dervishes,
so I can count you,
        claim you,
        calm you.

Hold still,
so I can draw you,
          close,
we aren't the first
to do this.

The Man Who Prints Eyeballs
(for Keith)

The man who prints eyeballs
has blue orbs himself.
Ol' Blue Eyes, I call him, on a good day.
On a bad day, little is said,
his blue speaking to my brown
dilating to black; the crook of his finger
indicative of where my chin should reside.

I have bathed his tonometer
in a cup of tears, at least, maybe
even a beaker full of salty fears.
'Good for you,' he used to say,
when I obeyed unquestioningly;
less of that now,
less of the Irish lilt,
the old jokes writhe feebly on the ground.

A laser beams into the core of me
as I pray for erudition,
but I retain only the briefest of facts:

>   a novel technique of bio-printing,
>   an ink jet recreating layers,
>   of ganglion and glial cells,
>   from the retina of a rat.

I wish I were a rat, I think.
But I don't. Not really.
I wish I were his guinea pig.
But do I? Really?

The man who prints eyeballs
is also an architect, an engineer,
and a local construction worker;
his site: the parameters of my cornea,
he measures in millimetres.

But on the weekends, he stretches out
into the bay of horizons,
unfurling wind and surf,
seeing nothing, hearing only
the song of seagulls

gathering him in.

Sunday Sweep

My floaters fall like dust moats
across the cortex of my eyes;
my humors break, and make
pictures, dancing shadows, light.

Sunbeams shaft through Winter's green
and bare brown leaves;
I pass through rooms, a silent ghost,
gathering dreams.

Bare feet and cloudy sight,
half whole and half unknown;
my hair a mess of springy curls,
my pen, my soul, at home.

I took the quiet road

Nirbhaya
(for Jyoti)

I am not here today
for I was never born
and I can never die.

I am not here today
in this ordinary form.

I am particle
and consciousness
in someone else's sky –

                                        I am wings

                                               I am flight

and this body
will surely die.

Tattered Wings

A butterfly up close
has tattered wings
and feather thin skin;
a fey, unnatural thing.

In flight,
it commands the skies;
all white, bright,
dancing light.

Blade of Green
(for James)

Give me just this blade of green,
beneath the scorching sun.

Give me just that trilling bird,
his dainty perch, his last of the summer fun.

Give me just this daily breath,
this curling autumn sleeve.

Give me just this barefoot right,
my fingers on a blade of green.

A Poet Said

I took the quiet road,
oh! so many miles ago.
I'll wait out the storm,
here where it's warm,
and shelter you with my smile.

Airplanes come and trains go by
and cycles whistle past me.

Sometimes I'll run to catch the bus
of chaos and the buzz;
hang on to the railing,
cool breezes, I'm sailing,
if only for a while.

Here I'll stop, here I'll rest,
or there by the lilac scent.
'Do not go gentle,' the poet said,
but it couldn't have been me
he meant.

After the Rain
(my mother said)

If you look outside the window
you can see a blackbird
washing itself
in a puddle.

Come quick!

Oh –

      it's gone.

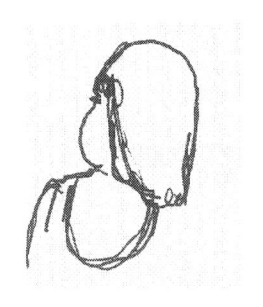

About The Author

Shaista Tayabali was born in Bombay, India, and now lives and writes in Cambridge, England. She is the author of the blog *Lupus in Flight* www.lupusinflight.com. Having completed a memoir, she is currently working on her first novel.